AF114371

Between the Spaces

Poetry by K.M. Herbert
Illustrations by Sussi Louise Smith

Text copyright © 2022 by K.M. Herbert
Illustration copyright © 2022 by Sussi Louise Smith
All rights reserved, including the right of reproduction in whole or in part in any form.

First published 2022

ISBN
978-1-80352-180-0

For you
For Nicholas and David
For all the spaces we call home

Preface

When I needed an illustrator for this poetry collection, I knew Sussi's whimsical and playful style would be just perfect. I proposed the idea to her; can you paint these poems? She was crazy enough to say yes. And I'm so glad she did, because the best part about this collection was the friendship that formed in its making. We spent 12 months working on this together, meeting at cafes and working in her garden. The end product was more than I could have imagined. 12 magical cards, unbound and untethered, just like the time in which they were written. We published the collection in May 2019 with just a small print run. We sold out and we moved on. I packed my cards away in a box. Covid happened. I published my first novel. Sussi published her first poetry collection. The world moved on.

And then on a muggy August morning in 2022, I went searching for those cards. I found them, loose and brilliant. The colours jumped out to me. The words felt familiar. But they meant something different than how I remembered them. That adolescent betweenness I had written about a decade earlier no longer felt so foreign or far away. In some ways, the words reminded me of who I was. In other ways, they reminded me of who I'd never be. I knew then they needed a new home.

In this strange post-pandemic world, we're all emerging from the spaces between who we thought we were and who we are, where we thought we'd be and where we're going. I hope these poems of colour and words bring you some comfort as they did to me. This time, civilised and bound, held together to be cradled by your hands, reminding you that you are not alone.

Yorkshire, September 2022

Contents

Preface	i
Stones and leaves	2
Spoken	4
Ours was a friendship	6
Empty mirror	8
We are trees	10
The silence	12
Gypsy	14
My sisters	16
Spaces	18
Love letter	20
Between dawns	22
Hills	24

Stones and leaves

Stones and leaves
once told me this would
be an old road too,

that the present would cement
in some embrace, an echo
unheard in open space.

They're nothing now,
the wet leaves underfoot,
trapped between stone,

but I picture them as they were:
falling from the faerie's ash
with ribbons in its branches –

caught in the wind and
away from home, in a world
they can never have.

I'm falling like the leaves,
before they touch stone,
falling in the space between,

suspended in the air
and yet – this stone too
will be my old and new.

Spoken

I've stumbled over
a precipice and I'm falling
like Alice and no one else has fallen
before me.

A noose waits to snap my reality,
with a body I used to be
hung in the past,

but I have ridden past places,
and I've blurred windows at night –
I have waited for the light.

Here are my words:
Hear my words.

Can you hear them?
I've made them for you.

Ours was a friendship

Ours was a friendship that needed no words.
Next to each other in green valleys
we'd listen for our breath, like soft
swells of green hills expanding in the sun.

Ours was a friendship that had its own speech:
a vocabulary within our irises
that knew when we needed to hide
or run or find a tale to cover our truths.

Ours was a friendship played along river beds,
placing dishes for fairies that would never come
and building bridges that could just carry
the weight of our small feet.

Ours was a friendship spent building worlds,
in the backdrop of reds and yellows,
against the ancient trees that call us home
to wash the dirt from our hands.

Ours was a friendship that ended
when we could no longer hold our hands,
when our bodies brought us shame and
our shared baths became unclean.

Ours was a friendship lost
in starburst branches, scattered
against the sky – golden glows dancing
in the autumn sun that cradle our lost fruit.

Ours is a friendship trapped in time,
a beat in Blake's song,
pressed in pastoral rhyme –
a golden twilight of summertime.

Empty mirror

I got high in Austrian castles where
the smoke from aristocratic lips
filled my head with fancy things.

The castle is cold but the
fire from my fingertips trail
smoke that follows me to

stone walls with tapered tapestries,
paintings piled in leaning stacks,
boxed romances in rooms.

And in daylight
her centre fountain is
an empty mirror looking in.

I got high in Austrian castles
where aristocrats and star-suited
men smoked and played games.

We are trees

We are trees
battered back by wind
we carry our hearts to the sky

our leaves stretch for the
golden light of our potential
our roots are never bound by place

and when we're weighed down
by the branches of our choices
we break free – and soar.

The silence

My parents left because of the silence
and the smoking thurifer
that marked their sheets.

Like gypsies they bounced between
cities with promises and
nicotine-stained hands.

She crept between their windows,
forgotten letters, creased at corners,
and aged photographs of mice.

Until they wandered into hollows
and with childhood melodies
hummed their youth away.

No – I was not born under city lights.
    A new kind of silence for me,
          800 miles into the trees.

Gypsy

I make my crown from
uprooted daisies and the
songs I hum are from far off places.

My clothes tell stories
of ancient streets made of cobble
and the strangers that kept me safe in spaces.

I want to love you but
you kept a hand to the turf
and I was destined for the earth.

My sisters

My sisters and I
hide in hills that
sing of Lir

and make hearts
from spoiled leaves
to mop our fears.

My sisters and I
wrap our arms
around lost time

and weep for
the moments we never
had in rhyme.

My sisters and I
stand in thimbles
along prison stitches

and in the lonely
moon hours we
howl at her skies.

My sisters and I
burned our hands
up on Pendle

but they know
we can never die,
our songs never lie.

Spaces

Here's a story
of the spaces we created
in the wonder of our boredom,
where we went when the sun closed.

In a twilight garden
we stroked tall petals, fell
on sharp grasses
next to tombstones and made love.

We tried to find the sky
but clouds and bright lights
got in the way of our
tomorrows.

I wish we could take back
lost loves
lost hearts
lost souls

between the empty space of
our greatness and our sorrow,
and the precipice that
begged us to jump.

Love letter

My only love letter
is an unused map,
but when you come back,
I'm miles away, still finding home.

Your sweet touch shakes me,
the cool touch of my forehead
against this plane fills me.

I need to feel the shaky ground
roll beneath, watch the landscape
melt from my window, rocked asleep
along country rails.

I want to love you
like I love this world
but she cries for me,
she calls for me.

Between dawns

When I reach out to the empty
space next to me at night,
you're adjusting the temperature
of your stovetop.

And when your body rolls over,
you anticipate a soft tug of the duvet
but I'm a thousand miles away,
wiping bread crumbs from my plate.

In the wee hours of my morning
and the beginning of your night –
when you've begun your slumber
and I've started to stir at the morning light –

I imagine our breath begins to heave the same sigh
and our hearts pulsate to a familiar sound
and in that fine brightness before dawn
our souls return together to form one.

Hills

These hills were here
before me
and when I'm gone,
they'll be here
before you.

These trees too,
they tell us
things that were
and will be,

like the wind
carrying old songs
that will carry ours.

And when she calls
we are pulled to her,
into the inward pond

where you too will be pulled,
and in that tumbled embrace,
beneath her earthy core,

we are here
and home is near.

www.ingramcontent.com/pod-product-compliance
Ingram Content Group UK Ltd.
Pitfield, Milton Keynes, MK11 3LW, UK
UKHW060737060526
12295UKWH00007B/12/J